Codependency!

World, Change! So I Feel Better!

Brian Schulman

Table of Contents

Introduction

Codependency is a relatively new term that found its root in the study of addiction and the families of addicts. Melanie Beattie wrote the official canon, which depicts the original take on codependency, characterized by wives or husbands of addicts who found themselves unable to separate from the very painful relationship with an addict—and—in fact, mostly finding themselves trying to please and/or control the addict seemingly out of care for their husband. A series of behaviors and patterns of thinking were identified in the "co-addict" that presents as a "dis-ease" all its own: codependence, or, another version of the word: codependency.

The "co-addcit" found herself or himself hooked to the addict and really trying to make themselves feel better *as they stayed with the addict.* These behaviors are people-pleasing, guilt and shame throwing, anger and control, bargaining with the addict, counter-dependence, "tough love", deprivation, screaming and yelling, etc.

Through these behaviors, and the belief that they will "work" to solve the problem centered in the other person, the wife of the addict (or husband), likely unwittingly, entered into a binary vortex, a co-existence of pain instead of marital bliss, as real or limited as that may be—a binary vortex, like two object gravitating with each other in a really messed up orbit: a maintained dependence—but really owed in responsibility to oneself, not the addict. These behaviors and thinking all seemed to be about the addict. And society would probably co-sign this thinking for you. As everybody is pretty much codependent in very significant ways. And addicts are considered wrong generaqlly no matter what, as their disease is not yet recognized widely as such—as opposed to a selfish indulgence.

We all think largely according to how others think, perceive, perceive us, and, all the norms of our current society. We are all about façade and name and reputation, whether we realize it or not. And we all base our feelings and actions around others, those around us; and largely according to societal norms—despite greater wisdom. Thus, we are not the wisest of societies. But it really is "who we are" (so we think).

If one were to look at how wisdom changes over time, but is never recognized at the time by most, this point would be clearer, the world once having thought to be flat being the most popular example. Everyone thinks a certain way niw too—a largely codependent way—but thinks nothing of it—and we continue to create our

own suffering through this way of thinking unwittingly yet willfully.

Not to digress too far from this point, as it is crucial, still, most relationships, jobs, etc, do not have the extreme turmoil of other situations where a diagnosis is sought—or delivered—with or without the permission of the co-addict, the codependent. So we figure life is largely suffering; also ancient wisdom, if you want to call it that, so we don't really notice how messed up most of us really are. Because we are *normal*—meaning most people are like this. At least, we have nothing better to compare it to in a secular, materialistic world like "The West." So *it's all good*. Even though we feel way more pain than we need to: due to this stuff. But, with this knowledge; and the more outllying cases as indicators of what arc our life's plot is on, we can quickly identify dysfunctional patterns, maybe even before the DSM (the diagnositc and statistical manual for doctors) and our therapist.

But in some cases, a person's suffering is so great, that they go to a therapist or MD about it. And thus, codependency is now on the map (and a point on the graph for all of us— though we'll elaborate on that later). And the thinking and acting that goes into this pain is now being reassessed, though slowly as change is generally organic,(except when Afghani farmers attack the New York Police and Fire Departments (whether they realized it or not)).

These patterns of behavior, at first seeming to be outliers, have drawn significant attention in the therapeutic community as a newer disease, called codependence. This people-pleasing; this control through a number of means—to make oneself feel better—has now been identified as "codependency." *And, that these "codependents" are doing it to themselves—not in a blame way, like we do with the disease of addiction—but in a "you-can-move-towards-solving-your-own-pain" way.*

Kind of like they are doing subconsciously in their codependence, but in reverse.

So, really, the "co-addict" acts and thinks in these ways *to feel better themselves. And has nothing to do with anyone else:* the addict in their home, or family, or distant lineage, etc. or anyone else! Ever, though this one you may not believe until later. Every problem we have, we have been taught is about someone else; or something else, something we want, something we don't, or can't, have, etc. It, everything, still seems to be about someone (or something) else being your problem.

The "co-dependent" acts and thinks in these ways *to feel better themselves.*

Now this is the case with just about everything. So, one might say, it's not entirely abnormal. All people try to achieve a better life/outside world to feel better inside. So it's kind of sane. But its way overkill in most cases. Though not by conventional wisdom: the current common knowledge. In many way it's kind of not sane. But no one would say so, virtually. To change one's outside worlds to fit one's own desires: to varying degrees. It's an endless battle.

We really can't change people, places, and things that well. Thus we suffer quite a bit of the time. I mean changing the world to feel better seems a futile effort and, I would say, insane. And the amount that we try is probably inversely proportional to our inner peace. In other words, the more we have to try to fix our outside world, probably the less happy we are. This is codependency.

We, ourselves, *to feel better inside* ourselves, our own emotions, try to *control* our worlds, though sometimes subtle noticeably to ourselves. It's an act of finding solace through *control*, though often *control* through people-pleasing or deference; or guilt or shame or badgering—originally identified in an untenable situation: a co-habitation with an addict; a very difficult and painful place to be

(especially in a society that treats the disease of addiction the way many do: as criminals, liars, cheaters, and thieves (none of which is true, by the way, in societies where addiction is not criminalized or taboo. But the conversation on the failures and exacerbation of the policy of prohibition is saved for another book))

Thus, there is a broader and consistent pattern that defines codependency on its own—as opposed to just being a "co-addict:" There is thought a *taker and a giver (and we usually side with the giver, a good habit, but in this case a form of enabling—encouraging the co-addict, the codependent's disease— meaning co-signing their pain and suffering because we don't know any better).*

However, even being the *giver, the martyr,*

codependence is now recognized as a disease of its own. And many treatment centers for addiction are now trying to treat for codependency—along with a 12-step self-help group of its own (two actually) that exists. It could be, and in many circles *is*, considered an addiction of it's own.

But most still think that changing the world around you to suit yourselves, in its myriad of micro and *normal* forms, is sane and normal and *okay. It is okay to be affected/**controlled** by the emotions of those around you. It is okay to suffer over things in your world that go wrong everyday. "It is certainly not my fault." Thus, without realizing what we are putting* *ourselves through, it is **okay** to be*

***codependent**.*

True, it is not usually our fault that things go wrong in life—but it *is* our fault that we suffer as much as we do over it. Fault is not the ideal word. *Responsibility* is better. *Choice* is even better. Should we reach that place. Which, if you follow along, you can.

Selfish Love – The Bigger Problem

Most people grow up fantasizing about a perfect, romantic marriage, often with one of them "saving" the other or both of them "completing" each other. In our world there is rampant "codependence:" emotional dysfunction whereby people offer "love" and "support" to each other, appear to be caring, to themselves and others, but really are acting out of fear, selfishly attempting to control or determine the outcome of another's actions to feel better themselves. The desire on the part of those who act in these "need-based," "caring" relations, is to feel safe or okay based on the service they are performing for the other. This classically happens in some of the most dysfunctional relationships and family systems, but it is a plague in our society and in almost all human relations as we know them. Our legal systems are based on debt and guilt; our marriages are cages for our partners; our families are often controlling and petty, if not abusive or neglectful. Our work and peer relations are often fraught with competitive character assassination. Our good friendships are generally the only relationships we have that have a chance of being string and judgment-free.

When a codependent person acts for another, he or she subconsciously or consciously expects a certain result or response. They have learned over time, that a successful skill in getting their needs met is to shower affection or service on another, to the point that they live by a "system" of cause and effect that they depend on emotionally, even if it is a fear-driven or unstable system.

A hallmark of these types of relationships is one person "making" the other one feel guilty, through direct communication, or indirect body and emotional language. Of course, it is not just the ability of one to actually "make" the other feel guilty, but in the unhealthy dance of codependence—the dance of action and expected result. It works because both believe in the dance, or "system," that they ascribe to.

Listen to most of our love songs and romantic movies and you will notice that we are literally plagued to our great and collective dis-ease in almost all of our relationships by this selfish love. This can be annihilated in our lives— individually with concerted effort, and collectively as more of us join the ranks of those who instead ascribe to a freer love.

The Definition of Codependency

Definition 1. There are varying definitions of codependency. But, in essence,

> *It is the condition of a person acting, thinking, and feeling according to another or others to feel okay—and feeling okay only when others think or act a certain way.*

Instead of finding and acting in their own truth regardless of the people places and things around them. *And,* looking at it globally, it is rampant—a plague on most of the world that we know; affecting virtually all of us who are not self-actualized.

Definition 2. There is also the very strong element of

> *One's feeling state being determined by things outside themselves; anything outside themselves.*

This is a broader definition—and more in line with any addiction or behavioral dis-ease or dysfunction—and the human condition at present. This is the kind of stuff spirituality tries to get at—to ameliorate. From John Lennon and George Harrison to Miguel Ruiz currently.

The broader definition is indicative of many things that ail us. It is a very useful template to look at everything we do. Why do I suffer over everything around me? Why do I need to arrange my world to suit me—and, thus, why can't I ever be happy for long?—as the stars very rarely align to suit just us.

But the second definition, while it does address almost everything that ails us, is less useful as a definition for our purposes right now: a template to affect change and allow healing for those of us where *people and our relationship to them* is the issue.

That, specifically the subject of this book— and the understanding of codependence specifically for the benefit of those of us who suffer from it, as it is commonly understood: the first way.

This book being a medicine for codependency as we understand it. Particularly in the first way, the common viewpoint of it in the therapeutic community, and *the plague of our society that need be addressed—that of our addiction to people—and our belabored suffering over others' thoughts and actions.*

But looking at it through both definitions, and very much through the second definition by the end of this book, the solution will be quite evident and useful to us.

I am saying that virtually all of us are codependent; virtually all of us suffer from having our thoughts, feelings, motivations, and actions based on the thoughts, feelings, motivations, and behaviors of another or others in general. We are not okay when others do not act the way we want them to. We are not happy if our husband or wife is not happy. We change ourselves to meet the needs or dislikes or requirements of another or others—almost globally. It is bred into us from birth. Our music and movies reflect this tale—and create it again in each new generation, along with our parents, schools, and religions at times.

To a point, this is okay. Not preferable, but codependence in ways of less suffering and hurting, but *significantly functional ways* could be considered good or even necessary. Thus, to a point, feeling and acting according to those around you *without thinking too much about it—thus, with it being domesticated into you without your knowledge*—is the oil that allows the machine of our society to function normally and well without us having to think to much about it. We are bred to get along and function as partners, co-workers, and as a society. Codependency is a big part of this.

But outside of the **necessary** oil of the machine of society and relationship, codependence is tremendously hard and even deadly, at times. There have been real suicides over a girl or a guy or family, etc.

When you hear or feel that "you complete me," you see nothing wrong. When you think of relationship or marriage, you assume a set of rules that appease the other member of the relationship or yourself without even a second thought about the limitations and judgments contained therein. We are like kites in the breeze of others—whichever way they blow, we follow (even if we lead).

> *So what is the harm of codependency? Some of it seems obvious: we are less joyous and peaceful due to our wind-vane nature. And we make choices that do not benefit ourselves and those whom we care for based on this diseased pattern. We usually live 80 or 90 years in large part suffering for and from others—when we could have been okay within ourselves the whole time*

despite external circumstances. Some
even die from codependency. There are
many suicides and murders over "love,"
etc. And even if one doesn't die from
codependence, one does suffer a great
percentage of their life over the
thoughts, feelings, and actions of others.

But to be okay, and not suicidal, or in hell
much of the time, was a choice that we didn't
even know we had—to be happy or at least
okay independently.

People-Pleasing

People-pleasing is the hallmark of codependency. It is the condition where we adjust who we are to be okay by another. We change how we act according to those around us. It's hallmark is fear. Often of subconsciously remembered threat, danger, or perceived danger in formative years.

Some call it being a chameleon. An animal whose color changes to match the colors around them. Similarly, a codependent changes their personality depending on those around them. Sometimes their entire personality.

These people, people-pleasers, usually end up matched up with someone who exhibits this "father"-like anger or control. In many cases, an addict, or an abuser. As the people-pleaser naturally looks "up" at others. And, implicitly sees a hierarchy.

And in virtually all cases, someone who has a lot of healing to do. Or, the people-pleaser ends up wth someone "safe." Someone who poses no "heirarchcial" threat. In the classic case of Melanie Beattie, someone they can "help."

> *This heriarchy, by the way, is strongly present in all of our communities—large or small.*

But, really, we are seeking a familiar dynamic from our formative years, childhoods, etc., where we can feel the comfort of "the devil we know." We feel better, more accustomed, *and, believe it or not, more safe: in our familiarity; and familiar behavior comes much easier;* without us even realizing it—and that we might be able to be much happier.

> *Usually a codependent is a pleaser to feel safe.* As they were to be during their childhood.

As time goes on, the codependent finds their habit of pleasing makes them well-loved: *safe in their mind*—which a mind of *un-safety:* insecurity.

There may eventually even be the element of pride in self-sacrifice (martyrdom) in this activity. Or they are a nervous wreck. Or a "Saint" of some sort, as sometimes, society will reward this self-sacrifice; she or he is always "thinking of another."

Though self-sacrifice is, at best, a short circuit in our collective programming to be loving and caring to each other—a very good predisposition that many, if not most of us to feel automatically—and truly be good and add good to the world. But if one is truly codependent, where this "natural desire has far exceeded its truly good nature, and harms the codependent herself, or the addict, et al., then maybe some amending of ourselves, our

thinking, and behavior, for our (and others')
benefit.

Bargaining

An alternative to people-pleasing, with a little strength gained, is bargaining. It is a well-known early stage of grief processing. The stages mirroring many of our relations. And, perhaps, indicating that most of our relations are that of pain in large part.

When the people-pleaser gets a little smarts, she or he starts to try and bargain with their partner. Or friends. Or family. The first stage of denial is over. Denial of things being severely messed up in an addictive situation. And pretty normally messed up in general. So bargaining is the usual second strategy.

It could be called grief of losing one's husband. Or drug. Or job. Etc. It is an attempt to rescue the situation. To change things for the better. But it is giving oneself away, perhaps, even likely, giving too much of oneself in an effort to make things better. Not only does it not work usually. It also is one sort of handing over one's ovaries. Or whatever.

Not that compromise in a relationship is always bad—perhaps we could save the other half of the marriages with the dedication of our grandparents or wisdom in compromise and kindness of our own parents' generation (the 60's children); though it is those baby boomers that are having the most marriage issues now—

However, in most cases, conventionally, it is really giving oneself away. It would be considered an "endgame"/last-ditch effort—like appeasement pre-war in the 1930's—if it weren't for the fact that codependence is a disease (a plague in fact) and pain and suffering are what we are used too. And addiction and codependence are really bad diseases. One of which, yes, most of us have. And the other, these people demonize and lock away from sight.

So, for the codependent, bargaining is an early strategy. Though in the stages of grief one has already lost whatever one is still bargaining for—likewise here. If you are bargaining your self away, chances are you are not one of the "progressive" types where you have a pretty good marriage—and you are just trying to compromise on the vacation destination for winter break—or, god, forbid, you can admit when you are arong, save something extreme like cheating. But have self-awareness of your own baggage and that is what the discussion is about.

More likely, you are begging in a way for the other person to stop something horrible—or that "makes" you feel horrible. Or you are an intolerable personality yourself and you are trying to avert what is, to you, like nails on a chalkboard.

And, like they say in twelve step programs, we usually give up everything before we are willing to change. And have to reach a "bottom:" a really bad place to change significantly or entirely. This is the case with most behavioral diseases (addiction included) and is the case with codependency too. In the rooms of these twelve step programs, they ask, rhetorically, what is the definition of insanity, quoting Einstein. The answer is "repeating the same behavior expecting different results."

So, basically, in most relationships, we are insane (and by ourselves too, as we repeat the same things that bring us suffering whether there is a partner in crime or not). As we both do the same stuff, without awareness, that makes us unhappy—both parties. *And* we try and change the other person again and again, as we will further delineate in this book.

So we try and bargain. If I..., will you stop ...
(drinking, abusing me, abusing the kids, all the
way to watching B movies instead of spending
tme with "me"). But, as half our marriages
dissolve, bargaining usually does not work.

And in codependency, there is a real fire
under our rears to bargain. So we are not
even even-keel when we are bargaining. We
will pull out all the stops and sell our soul,
basically, at least for a while, to try and change
the other person: read *feel better—and* keep
our wife. Or friend. Or job. Etc.

As if it were not okay to be alone. Or take a
stand. Not necessarily by yelling. Just setting
a boundary. And being able to keep our
integrity—if we even know what that means—

and not sell it for the temporary feeling of security.

But really we are *very* attached to something. Usually a person. *And we are not okay without them—and* with them acting the way they do. *So it continues...*

Blame

Anytime we say "you make me feel...," "you hurt me," "you made me angry," etc., we are, in essence, disowning our feelings and putting the blame on others. Our feelings are the primary way that we are codependent. From them comes our behaviors.

We live in a society that promotes or cosigns blaming others for the way you feel. And what is the response? "I'm so sorry" or "you deserve it because...."

> Never "your feelings are your own—and mine my own."

A good way to remember this—and practice it—is to become aware of your feelings, become aware of the thoughts about them, and to start every confrontation or conversation about your feelings having to do with another or others by reciting

"When you [specific, observable, action/words], I feel [feeling]." As opposed to "you make me feel …" or some grand abstract like "you drain me.

"For example, "when you monopolize the television, I feel angry"—instead of "you make me angry with your lack of care for me." Because he does not actually make those feelings in your body. They result from your own inner entanglements and beliefs and emotional body.

We truly are independent beings emotionally or mentally if we practice. And there are probably a lot of layers of ways we implicitly, though unwittingly, understand each other, with a lot of abstracts, beliefs, and blame and harbored resentment—leading to fights that can't be won, pain that can't be explained, thus solved, a lot of fighting, etc...

This type of practice will begin to untangle our web of painful comprehension and understanding and pain (whether the other party participates or not). And relief is on the horizon.

Guilt and Shame Throwing

When a codependent has had enough, things get uglier. After a while, even the classic people-pleasing codependent gets angry. For the addict (or insert other person here)—*and* the codependent. But not in outright control. For they are still afraid. And still working within the confines of *normalcy*. Thus, guilt and shame throwing. Normal ways of being healthy in relationship. The people-pleaser, after a while, starts to throw barbs; to find holes in the armor of another. The codependent is gaining strength and can start to be mean too.

Thus, the second trait of codependency. Does guilt and shame throwing solve the problems in the relationship. Well, its one of the ways we "get along," cosigned by the other person. ("Yes I am guilty, I'm sorry, I'll change," etc..)

So throwing pain felt *does* fix some things— sometimes. Not usually in addiction, but in most relationships. *Fix* being changing another's behavior (instead of your own—so *you* feel better). The other person has to agree. And now your pain is his pain too. But your pain is lessened. But guilt and shame are increased. And now, he can use that too on you. Now you are in a dynamic where it is okay to use pain to solve problems. Or at least increase pain on one or both parts. But we kinda like it. Like the pain around sex and sexual relations being *good* for us.

But we are still in the binary gravity of the relationship. We are still basing ourselves off another. And the new option of guilt and shame throwing still hurts. Though one starts to feel fire in their veins. And that is a high unto itself. As a society, we are addicted to suffering most of the time. which means we like to do painful things and be in pain. We almost all utilize anger and fear, though they are a dictatorship unto themselves—even within ourselves. Yet we love this. It fits the heirarchy model that most of us observe implicitly. And it is the general condition of our planet (wars, slavery, economic exploitation, etc); and we do the same things on a micro, personal level. And, I hate to tell you: we implicitly cosign this world by being this way. Much less trying to help. To heal the world. Or the addict. Or ourselves.

Anger and Control: "Tough Love"

Eventually—or initially—one has the inclination to rage. Be it through actions or voice. Either the codependent has had enough (but can't get away *still*—in action or words) or we are the type of person who thrives off of anger, fear, and what most refer to as "tough love." And as we are all tough. And love toughness. And the other person is wrong (always). Tough love is *in*. In fashion. In style. Not in the diagnostic manuals or ethics of caregiving or relationship books. But in conventional *wisdom*.

Addiction counselors and family therapists of addicts often teach it. Though the recovery rate in addiction is among the worst of all diseases. PhD's usually do not teach it. Friends and most other *normal* people co-sign it, if one even needs that cosigned. But toughness—anger—is the truth the light and the way in general. We rarely get that rush, unless we are at war and get to watch bullets and bombs laser strike their targets. God bless the news and media magnates.

But the rush of power or retribution does not solve many problems. Though it makes us feel right. I mean we *are* right. So it makes sense.

But either we love that firepower and fire in our veins or we don't really know how to be healthy or helpful. Penance envy is quite the addiction. And another form of ones own feeling better now at the cost of another—and still based on another: still trying to solve our need for a valium, for example, as an answer to another's taking of too much valium, etc: Hurt or abandon the other person to feel better.

In addiction recovery circles this is called taking the poison, oneself, of anger to hurt another—and I'll add "or *help* the other." It happens even in Al Anon; and long after one's partner is not an addict any longer. *And it is another form of codependence* (and stage of grief—*reaction to something that one cannot change*).

Counter-dependence

The pinnacle for a codependent is counter-dependence. Finally being free of people pleasing. Being free of others. Being able to *be themselves*. Being mean.

Counter-dependence is kind-of the opposite of codependence, as its name indicates. It is a condition and a conditioning wherein we make sure to *not* be dependent in any way we can on another. Sometimes evident by oddly energized conflict. But really a condition where one has to be entirely independent.

The dis-ease here comes where we still base our actions on another. But in an opposite way. The rebel or the goth or the alternative cultural is *different than "the norm". And they love it.*

Not that there aren't many normal things to virtue being different than. Though in a predictable way—as some have to be opposite of *something*. And they often or usually find a group to be like too—in their *different* way.

But, externally motivated or not, it just means that internally we are in *total* control of our own experience and the resultant choices and behaviors. It may be associated with anger. Or former people-pleasing/codependency. Which may come from old wounds or abuse. Still potentially diagnostic. And potentially painful. As much be obvious to an onlooker.

But not so much to the counter-dependent herself.

But, as with everything, it is *almost always obvious to the onlooker,* **though the onlooker becomes pretty blind when looking in the mirror.**

Conclusion

Does this mean that we are to be anti-social or "counter-dependent" (to have a pattern or origin of behavior that arises from a counter reaction to others and my original codependency to recover from codependence: to be the opposite of codependent)?

Or get an immediate divorce?

Or get "a black belt in Al Anon?"

Or isolate from the ills of the world?

Well, it's just about getting well. It's about awareness, first, as with every self-healing. Then adjusting accordingly. Just knowing oneself without fear running the show (need for this or that unnecessarily: a feeling here or there; all the way to an unhealthy marriage). It's about living in freedom to be okay. Just to be okay. Whether things are okay or not. Knowing that there is something inside of you that is above the fray: regrettably, above-normal.

It's about not trying to change the word to feel better ourself; in others, in everything. Feelings pass. Thoughts often lie. People always fail us eventually. But so do we fail ourselves.

And we really can only change ourselves in any permanent, lasting way that would significantly ameliorate our suffering—lead to our happiness. Though this self-healing **will** have a ripple effect. In our little world.   And the more of us that do it—especially in love— a ripple effect on the world.

It's about knowing oneself and one's true needs and self. Not the self that was handed to us by others who had their hide handedto them too. But a self that fears not. A self that knows she's okay no matter what. Thus does not need to change another. Or anything. Then can manipulate one's life much more *liberally*. In love and freedom. Not fear and anger or scarcity.

Love, compassion, kindess, ease, comfort. Not the right couch or apartment, or the right response from another—not to mention always having to micromanage another—but also having the right point of view. Not the right lover. The right love. And that you already have: you!

And that attracts less pain and strife. And drama. And that is more attractive too.